YoungWrit...

WONDER VERSE

Young Wordsmiths

First published in Great Britain in 2025 by:

YoungWriters® Est. 1991

Young Writers
Remus House
Coltsfoot Drive
Peterborough
PE2 9BF
Telephone: 01733 890066
Website: www.youngwriters.co.uk

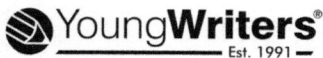

FOREWORD

WELCOME READER,

For Young Writers' latest competition *Wonderverse*, we asked primary school pupils to explore their creativity and write a poem on any topic that inspired them. They rose to the challenge magnificently with some going even further and writing stories too! The result is this fantastic collection of writing in a variety of styles.

Here at Young Writers our aim is to encourage creativity in children and to inspire a love of the written word, so it's great to get such an amazing response, with some absolutely fantastic pieces. This open theme of this competition allowed them to write freely about something they are interested in, which we know helps to engage kids and get them writing. Within these pages you'll find a variety of topics, from hopes, fears and dreams, to favourite things and worlds of imagination. The result is a collection of brilliant writing that showcases the creativity and writing ability of the next generation.

I'd like to congratulate all the young writers in this anthology, I hope this inspires them to continue with their creative writing.

CONTENTS

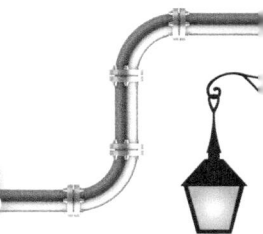

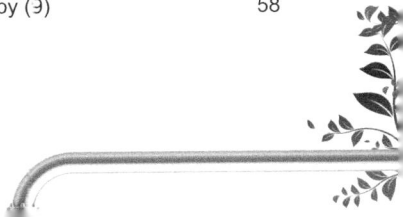

Mia White (9)	59
Nitya Seechurn (8)	60
Kaden Turner (8)	61
Arthur Higgs (8)	62
Jessica Hillsdon (9)	63
Frankie Lewis (9)	64
Roman Smith-Chester (8)	65
Florence Payne (8)	66
Hang Wong (8)	67
Layla Mullins (9)	68
Luke Murphy (9)	69
Scarlett Morgan (9)	70

Hartsfield JMI Primary School, Baldock

Max E (11)	71
Lottie R (11)	72
Betsy Fletcher (11)	73
Milly Reynolds (11)	74
Adam Fixter (10)	75
Max R (11)	76
Annabelle White (11)	77
Luna Constantinou (11)	78
Beth Sutton (11)	79
Arthur Keay (11)	80
Cyril (11)	81
Olivia Raheja (11)	82
William Cartwright (10)	83
Marley Banks (10)	84
Oscar Richards (11)	85
Leo M (11)	86
Harry M (11)	87
Sam Vall (11)	88
Lacie Waldock (11)	89
Harrison Parker (10)	90
Martha (11)	91
Sadie Evans (11)	92
Eli Kendall (11)	93
Lily-Mae Furse (11)	94
Isabel (11)	95
Bradley (11)	96
Barnaby Reid (11)	97
Labella McCarthy (11)	98

Rex Willett (11)	99
Harry H (11)	100
Lottie Haden (11)	101
Joni Martin (11)	102
Alexander DT (10)	103

Kennington Primary School, Fulwood

Zaynab Shah (10)	104
Inayah Qazi (10)	105
Zayn Sheth (10)	106
Muhammad Amin Bhura (10)	107
Safiyyah Alam (10)	108
Aizah Khalid (10)	109
Ali Ayub (10)	110
Mustafa Ayub (10)	111
Mohammed Hassan Shaikh (9)	112
Naad-e-Ali Kazmi (10)	113
Ayesha Bargit (9)	114
Zahraa Harif (9)	115
Zeyad Patel (10)	116
Rumaisah Matki (10)	117
Isa Pepi (10)	118
Isa Wadee (10)	119
San Rassul (10)	120
Zidan Khandia (10)	121
Samuel Hamilton-Gray (9)	122
Amina Hussain (9)	123

Linton Mead Primary School, Thamesmead

Tiffany Monford (10)	124
Elizaveta Nikulina (10)	126
Daena Julia Castro (10)	127
Imogen Mulheran (10)	128
Rayan Mesbah (9)	129
Henry Sadagos (10)	130
Maleeah Grima (9)	131

Rosetta Primary School, London

Aliyah Hatab (9)	132
Lana Tahmim (8)	133
Afnan Arifi (9)	134
Zara Munsha (9)	135
Haider Ali Asad (9)	136
Alicja Borzecka (8)	137
Ieva Kalinauskaite (9)	138
Fedora Naniwono (9)	139
Ziad Haidari (9)	140
Nana Aba Dzigbodi (9)	141
Sreyansh Aryal (8)	142
Arissa Ahmed (9)	143
Avayah Pierre (9)	144
Lara Zenti (9)	145
Mateo Hernandez (8)	146
Amaya Sahni (9)	147
Marsad Mohammed (8)	148
Zaid Shariff (9)	149
Reynaldo Augustine Gatchalian (8)	150
Kevin Chen (9)	151
Rayan Dohlal (9)	152
Azhaan Chowdhury (9)	153
Evie Bonnett (8)	154
Adeeb Rahman (9)	155
Adam Kessira (9)	156
Mila Saber (9)	157
Alexandra Tiganescu (9)	158
An Gia Nguyen (9)	159
Cristhofer Pachon (9)	160
Elijah Nuamah (9)	161
Elissa Hassan (9)	162
Mohammed Zayaan Hussain (9)	163
Donnie Marsh (9)	164
Rhema Odede (9)	165
Clinton Osakwe (9)	166
Leo Munroe (9)	167
Keyaan Aryan Earla (8)	168
Billy Ferrier (8)	169
Lyza Reddin (9) & Tre Guy (8)	170
Jayzon Philpot Pierre (9)	171
Maddison Candler (9) & Bernice	172
Deniz Nazim Gursul (9)	173

Sandbrook Community Primary School, Rochdale

Hikmah Lawal (9)	174
Mohamed Barry (9)	175
Amelia Khan Speak (9)	176
Alyaannah Shaikh (9)	178
Raza (9)	179
Hanan Mudassar (9)	180
Nevaeh-Rose McCulloch (9)	181
Holly Holmes Smithes (9)	182

Shevington Vale Primary School, Appley Bridge

Ella Yates (10)	183
Rosa Blinkhorn (9)	184
Sophia Koskinas (9)	185
Niamh Latham (10)	186
Ollie Anderson (10)	187
Lucy Lavery (10)	188
Madison Ascroft (9)	189
Blake Bristow (10)	190

Wath Victoria Primary School, Wath Upon Dearne

Labeebah Odumosu (9)	191

THE CREATIVE WRITING

Gods And Goddesses Of The World

These are the amazing gods of Rome
Have you heard of Poseidon? He's brighten;
You may have heard of Zeus, but he's not juice.
Medusa stares at you as you turn to stone.

Heard of Hades, he's not a group of ladies;
Heard of Aphrodite, she's almighty;
Heard the underworld, it swirled, Hades is led.
These gods are Greek, not clique, they're not bled, so

What crazy gods, they all tell a story;
They say hi when they're passing by, don't mind.
Tell a different story of their part
The gods are special, but they're not blinded

They're all gods, they're saying hi, don't mind them.
Freya is a kind, pretty, shimmering gem.

Ruby-Mae Chant (11)
All Saints Church In Wales Primary School, Llanedeyrn

1

Legends Of Old Trafford

In the heart of Manchester, where the Red Devils play,
Lived heroes and legends who lit up the day.
With chants in the air and the fans on their feet,
The Theatre of Dreams held glory and heat.

Cantona came with collar held high,
A king with a stare and fire in his eye.
He went past defenders with swagger and pride,
Scoring with magic no one could hide.

Then came young Beckham, with boots laced in gold,
A right foot so deadly, brave and bold.
From halfway, he struck, the crowd held their breath,
As the ball flew in, and stunned them to death.

Giggs on the wing, a flash of pure pace,
Twisting and turning, a blur in the race.
He weaved through the field like wind through the trees,
With moments of magic that brought teams to their knees.

Scholes with the thunder, a master of strike,
Passed with perfection, no one alike.
A general silence, calm and so wise,
He'd score from afar and dazzle the skies.

Together they battled, in red they bled,
Chasing the titles and charging ahead.
They lifted the cups, they made the world cheer,
United with passion, year after year.

So here's to the legends, the glory, the might,
Who gave us magic on cool Friday nights.
Old Trafford remembers, its echoes still sing,
Of Beckham, of Cantona, and each football king.

Isla Winston (10)
All Saints Church In Wales Primary School, Llanedeyrn

Wild Colour

The rainbow parrots soaring so high,
Flying majestically through the sky.

The mandrill monkey so bold and bright,
Always ready to start a fight.

The frog so small but poisonous to all,
Which makes him feel so very tall.

The mantis shrimp, so full of colour,
Deep under the sea, makes others look duller.

The tiger so powerful, hunting its prey,
Never stopping, all through the day.

The peacock dancing through the forest,
Playing its own flying chorus.

From jungle deep to mountain tall,
In sky, the sea, and meadow small,

The animals play, they run, they sing –
Their colours paint the world like spring.

Molly Willetts (9)
All Saints Church In Wales Primary School, Llanedeyrn

The Spirits

Quick! The boy is now finally asleep,
The wisps wander around the house with glee.
Out come the spirits, in the hall, they creep,
"Oh my word!" they say. "We're finally free!"

The wisps are like a glowing ball of ice,
The spirits, like a human-based creature.
They fly, they twirl, they do it again twice,
They might even see you in the future.

Next time you see a wisp, keep an eye out,
Be quiet, they only come out at night.
Even when you see a spirit, don't shout,
Carefully, please don't make them have a fright!

They just come out of the darkest of night,
Do not dare to scare them, please be polite!

Eloise Norman (11)
All Saints Church In Wales Primary School, Llanedeyrn

Fairy Dreams

Shining, shimmering rocks lie on the moss.
Secret door in the tree, fairies fly free,
Walk down to the lake to find a rock to toss.
Far away, you can hear buzzing bees,

Above the hills, where quiet shadows lie.
High above, sweet chirping sounds start to ring,
Find a fairy door, stop by and say 'hi'.
Far away, you can hear the town bell ding,

Moonlight shines, stars sparkle, animals lie.
Shimmer, sparkle, shine, every night until nine,
High above, birds of prey hunt every day.
Bright stars are worth more than a bright, shiny dime,

Sweet chirping sounds from the birds high above.
Shining, shimmering crystals you will love.

Georgina Hooper (11)
All Saints Church In Wales Primary School, Llanedeyrn

The Tree Seed

A little seed was buried in the ground,
And so the other clouds began to start.
It started raining since the seed was around,
That seed turned into a plant that needed art.

Soon, the little seed turned into a tree,
But soon that tree would not be standing right.
The big chainsaw made the tree want to flee,
But it was too late, and the tree saw light.

The tree was chopped down, and it became planks.
The wooden planks were carried like a mouse.
The planks were put onto a van like banks,
Each plank was carried up a hill to the house.

Once a little seed, now something else big,
All this would not have happened if not for the dig.

Alex Feay (11)
All Saints Church In Wales Primary School, Llanedeyrn

A Field Of Dreams, A Game Of Hope

The legendary sport where GOATs are born,
The mystic game where goals add to the cart,
This beautiful game we know and adore,
Wake up, we can make this big journey start.

He walked and walked until he found this ball,
"Don't worry," it said, "come and play, it's fun!"
It was a trap that had led him to fall,
It led to a pitch, shiny like the sun.

A pitch like none, full of hope and pressure,
A game full of hope, becoming a pro,
After this great sport, it will be fresher,
He was the best, though his chances were low.

This is a story of how you'll become,
The best football player in the outcome.

Zak O
All Saints Church In Wales Primary School, Llanedeyrn

The Keepers Islands

As the highlands glide across the large sky,
Because this is our big gliding highlands.
The air parade begins to play and fly,
And we are the only floating islands.

On a reef, there's a grand beach of vast sand,
On top of our isles, there are very white clouds.
Because in our highlands we have big hands,
But sometimes we might have some crowds.

Inside the vast sky, garden flowers bloomed,
The shining, sparkling sun shines brightly down.
Because this place is not supposed to be that doomed,
In the middle of all of it, there's a town.

This one guy called Kaiser is the reaper.
He protects us; he is our gatekeeper.

Oliver Taylor (10)
All Saints Church In Wales Primary School, Llanedeyrn

Natureland

The beaming hot sun glistens through the trees,
Lovely blue birds chirping so loud and proud.
The wind hits you just like a soft breeze,
In the clear skies, there is never a cloud.

The rivers flow across the gigantic rocks,
Insects are crawling, and the fresh smell of grass.
Creatures will roam like a fluffy, fierce fox,
Whilst a big, cold gust of air will blow past.

The lovely-smelling flowers glow in the light,
The crooked bridge looks above the river.
In the dark, creatures crawl in the night,
The cold water makes you want to shiver.

The moon comes up and the sun goes down,
No one can be let down by a bad frown.

Grace Heenan (11)
All Saints Church In Wales Primary School, Llanedeyrn

The Life In Space

The endless void, a canvas dark and vast,
With stars like diamonds, shining bright and light
A massive cosmic ocean, strong and fast,
Where new worlds form in flowing, starry bright.

Please open your eyes, it is not a dream.
The stars are just like bright shining diamonds.
You can watch the bright northern lights gleaming,
You must stay here even if it is for months.

You will have lots of fun and see spaceships,
Following the mist around the big space.
You could even find a better space blip,
Stars explode and leave a beautiful trace.

This adventure will end with good glory,
So do not forget this was just a story.

Oscar Barrett
All Saints Church In Wales Primary School, Llanedeyrn

The Delightful Couple

The steaming sun gleams on her reflection,
The toasty sand cuddles him like a bear,
That pleasing ocean shows her perfection,
As their heavenly eyes look with a stare.

The charming fish harass them like guards,
As they fondle with tears down their hot eyes,
They loaf in the cooked sand, making love cards,
As they both stare at the fluffy white skies.

They build sandcastles on the comfy sand,
They grab their sandy fists with great fun and joy,
They run on the sand gripping hand by hands,
He leaps into the ocean like a boy.

The ocean is as frigid as freezing snow,
Why don't you come and have a shining glow?

Ellis Cumberbatch (11)
All Saints Church In Wales Primary School, Llanedeyrn

The Mysterious Football

A football, not of leather, stitched and round,
A field of dreams, where shadows softly play.
But born of whispers, in the silent ground,
And stars ignite, to light the football day.

Their goals, not scored, but in our hearts are caught,
Passing swiftly and heading up high,
The players move, a dream, a fleeting thought,
Underneath the widest, opening sky.

Young players learn and try as they compete,
Football, a game of strength and even grace
And victory joy, and even defeat,
This lively, competitive outer world space.

Oh, football, that joy it brings is so keen,
A sport that bands a very vibrant scene.

Xander Prince (10)
All Saints Church In Wales Primary School, Llanedeyrn

The Magic World

The glittering wand looks like stars above,
Till the end, I'm a wizard with magic.
Wish a woo, wish a woo, a spell of love,
I'm still a wizard, but I can be tragic.

So strong and powerful, I shall be feared,
Magic everywhere, close and close too late.
Very old-fashioned, has a long, grey beard,
In danger, danger! Do not go past, mate.

The purple and blue cloak looks like outer space.
In a wooden house, where am I? Who knows.
In the air, there is a magic airbase,
It shines cool crystal, all the time it glows.

Dirty and old, broken down, can't be done,
Finally at peace, time to rest and won.

Eli Denning
All Saints Church In Wales Primary School, Llanedeyrn

Flowers And Bees

It blooms, so soft, so delicate and tall,
It snuggles the bugs, as warm as a bed,
Pastel and neon, the petals are small,
But all of these bees are buzzing ahead.

Showing its anthers to attract the bees,
Waiting for pollen to be collected,
One by one, the bees fly and come to see,
Take it all and make sure it is connected.

Buzz, buzz! They came to their honey-filled hive,
The blue flower has done its wondrous job,
They flew down into it and knew they thrived,
Their colours are as bright as corn on the cob.

Yet their journey still carries on today,
This time, not one flower but a bouquet!

Imogen Norman (11)
All Saints Church In Wales Primary School, Llanedeyrn

The Starlight Zone

Imagine a forest, a mystic place,
The trees whisper, spreading the quiet word.
This place is beautiful no need for pace,
It's a magical space, no peep to hear.

Above the huge trees, beauty has arrived,
Eternal stars reaching the Earth's end.
Galaxy's flowing with years to survive,
Planets switch and slide, starting to make trends.

You'll come in with an overly big ache,
You run around feeling like a deep wound
Searching for the immense majestic lake,
Stars will reflect onto the clear water.

The vast starry sky, the dark, misty trees,
All will make you feel a great sense of ease.

Olivia-Mae Owen (11)
All Saints Church In Wales Primary School, Llanedeyrn

The Beyond Of Dreams

Brain-twisting wonders are all in your dreams,
Take a walk closer and you will find home.
Growling galaxies gather around streams,
The wonders and whispers have ruled the throne.

Shooting stars are flying across your eyes,
On a cloud, magic starts forming around.
You're in space, don't pace, no one will see sunrise,
The precious galaxies form like a town.

The orbit absorbs the bad energy.
The cosmic spirits all gather throughout.
Mystery UFOs race for a win,
The spirits dance rapidly, big with a shout.

You closed your eyes you woke up right here,
We say goodbye with a massive, loud cheer.

Maddie Peterson (10)
All Saints Church In Wales Primary School, Llanedeyrn

The Milky Way Whispers

Above all, the land lies a secret place,
Gold, mystic aliens seen upon Mars,
A whirlpool of magic when you find space,
When you look, you will see millions of stars.

The bright sky was like a marble effect,
Would you like to see the galaxies above?
Sparkle and shimmer, the stars will reflect,
When you see the whole place, you'll fall in love.

Shimmery, shiny stars floating up high,
The shooting stars, always a lovely sight.
Wondrous dreams that fly high into the sky,
It is impossible to reach the height.

The gazing stars that sparkle in the night,
The shimmering moon shines very bright.

Kaitlyn Grant (10)
All Saints Church In Wales Primary School, Llanedeyrn

The Galaxy Secrets

Above all, land lies a calm secret place,
The majestic galaxy shines so bright.
The shining purple-blue mist is called space,
The glittery sky shines at the sight.

Bright colours of space, they will never fade,
Whispers are spreading around the universe.
The stars are so bright you won't ever find shade,
Following the secret of the blue verse.

Up so bright, so high you can see starlight,
The galaxy brightens up in the sky.
Looping around the beautiful moonlight,
The stars are so bright, big and always high.

The listening grey sparks, glittery moon,
But the universe will see you soon.

Faith Nwamuo (10)
All Saints Church In Wales Primary School, Llanedeyrn

Starlit Secrets In Fairy Glades

The dream moon gleams above the moonlit sky,
It's one big party, it's one of a kind.
Magic comes out with a peek of an eye,
The fairies and tulips are hard to find.

Butterflies and fairies fly with a wish,
As the clock ticks, it's time for the party.
Teacups and cupcakes twirl with a light swish,
The fairies together sing all hearty.

Unicorn and ponies come together,
Gold glitter and stardust fall all around.
Mixing a magic potion forever,
Fairies, pixies and gnomes dance on the ground.

Now it's time to end my secret old tale,
Fairies and gnomes say bye to the old snail.

Isabella Gonzalez (10)
All Saints Church In Wales Primary School, Llanedeyrn

Life Inside A Famous Painting

The wavy brush stroke feels silky and calm,
The way you look at it feels unreal.
When you could feel the magic in your palm,
It feels so nice, so calm, and so real.

The mountains point sharply at the bright moon,
Over the house, massive mountains do peek.
Beautiful shadows come over at noon,
Look at the mountains, you can't even speak.

With stars that are as yellow as the sun,
The sky is as blue as the ocean waves.
You feel trapped in a dream with everyone,
You will be surprised that there are no caves.

When you wake up, it feels like a weird dream,
It is never what you would seem.

Lexi-Rae Wyatt (10)
All Saints Church In Wales Primary School, Llanedeyrn

Beneath The Starlight Throne

The willows murmur secrets through her mind,
Tulips and orchids kiss her silky skin.
Everything is pristine, like gold refined,
Gleeful tears fall lovingly down her chin.

The sky, a canvas painted with starlight,
She sways in step with the weeping cherries.
The moon's gentle gaze shines oh so bright,
Her stare lands on the elegant fairies.

The great feel of magic, a thread of fate,
A secret unknown, a world beyond the veil.
Wonder blossoms, this story cannot wait,
Come and join our bewitching fairy tale.

With graceful eyes, watch the story unfold
Step into the best story ever told!

Vanessa Okafor
All Saints Church In Wales Primary School, Llanedeyrn

Part Of A Bigger Life

As the bluebird sings high up in the sky,
The bats flap about, and the owls concur.
Little frog jumps around, and the bees fly,
Catching pollen in their bright, bold, rich fur.

Baby fox cub is a curious guy,
The aardvark is fine with taking a stroll;
But bunny would rather stay in his sty,
The horse is too scared because he is just a foal.

Komodo dragon, well, he is a giant,
Great alligator, now he is colossal;
Yet a house cat can be quite defiant,
A cat is its own man; do not think it is docile.

Do not kill these poor animals, do not be rife,
Because we are all part of a bigger life.

Owen Belcher (11)
All Saints Church In Wales Primary School, Llanedeyrn

Life Of Mythical Creatures

The mythical creatures lie in the dark,
The vampire cannot come out in sunlight.
The chupacabra has a scary bark,
The skinwalkers lurk in the deep, dark night.

Griffins guard their possessions and treasure,
Mermaids lure sailors with enchanting songs.
A werewolf will get you under pressure,
While the birds listen to the sound of gongs.

The taotie serves warning against greed,
Fairies signify love, magic and death.
All the deer symbolise peace, a good deed,
Zombies and skeletons can't take a breath.

Bigfoot's biggest fear is a scary fire,
Dolus and Pseudologoi are liars.

Joshua Wilson (10)
All Saints Church In Wales Primary School, Llanedeyrn

Mythicality

The mythical creatures live in the night,
The dragon protects its diamonds and gold.
The griffin waits for the break of daylight,
And banshee's white light shines so perfectly and
boldly.

The phoenix light is so red and so light,
A Basilisk's fang is full of venom.
The Cyclops' bait quivers with some dark fright,
A skinwalker uses fur as denim.

If you hurt a Hydra it will double,
A kitsune never gets stuck in a hedge.
A Basilisk swims with gurgling bubbles,
Be absolute you don't slip off the edge.

When you look around the mythical bends,
Make sure creatures don't take your happy end.

Mia Sheen (11)
All Saints Church In Wales Primary School, Llanedeyrn

The Vibrant Beyond

High up in space, shimmering shiny light,
Round, beautiful, grey, silvery full moon.
The burning sun looked perfect in sight,
The moon looks like a big round balloon.

Above all the stars, there was an amazing space,
Stars quietly whispering like a dream.
Let's go around and find a peaceful place,
The sun glistened brightly like a gleam.

Astronauts fare lying mostly everywhere,
Terrifying, enormous, the black hole.
Careful because they could give you a scare,
Travelling to space was everyone's goal.

Flying around in the creepy midnight,
In space, it can be a joyful delight.

Charlotte Bulmer
All Saints Church In Wales Primary School, Llanedeyrn

Threads Of Infinity Between Galaxies

Above all skies carry a secret place,
Majestic creatures all in the starlight.
The pink and purple mist is called space.
The glazing sky shimmers in the moonlight.

Whispers within stars held a mystery,
Looping all around the galaxy twice.
Planets float above, making history,
Welcome to your wonderful paradise.

Space is endless, the colours never fade,
The galaxy shines within the light.
Galaxies are blooming in every shade,
A whole different universe, so bright.

That's where the galaxy lies to this day,
Now the galaxies are far, far away.

Layla Parker (9)
All Saints Church In Wales Primary School, Llanedeyrn

Animal Love

I love the turtles with their hard shell
I love the beautiful dolphins, underwater, they dwell
I love the polar bear with a fluffy coat and sharp claws
I love the fearless lions with deadly teeth in their jaws
I love the elephants with their long trunk and flappy ears
I love the cute and adorable puppies, they bring me to tears
I love the head-turning owls that appear at night
I love the bright orange tiger with amazing eyesight
I love all these animals; they mean so much to me
Let's look after these animals so they can be free.

Arya Higgins (9)
All Saints Church In Wales Primary School, Llanedeyrn

Our Incredible World

Birds flying in the sky,
Swooping and diving way up high,
Vibrant colours, flapping wings,
Melodies move as they sing.

Land animals are up next,
And some people say they are the best,
Leaping, running, prowling, too,
Chasing prey as they go through.

Sea animals are lurking in the waters so deep,
Fish swim, dolphins leap,
Turtles glide, sharks hunt,
People watch from the oceanfront.

This is our wonderful world!

Robyn Evans (9)
All Saints Church In Wales Primary School, Llanedeyrn

A Good Friend

A good friend is someone who
Wants to care
They share their stuff
To be kind
Sometimes in my
Mind
The words fly out from the brain
I say, "That's great."
Every school day I see
Her
I'd prefer a friend like
My BFF
Than a rude
BFF.

Niralaya Naresh Kumar (11)
All Saints Church In Wales Primary School, Llanedeyrn

The Stars Glisten

The stars glisten
The bright shooters
Scattered around the galaxy
Joining dots to paint a story
Maybe one for
You and me
Let's think
Think
And watch them wink
Smiles begin to burst
Happy dancers shining in the dark sea
Don't you see?

Zachary Belcher (9)
All Saints Church In Wales Primary School, Llanedeyrn

Monster

Monster, as hairy as a wolf
And as white as a cloud
He is quiet
The opposite of bad
He loves hugs and is soft too
He will say hi instead of bye
And I think he will love you too, monster.

Nia Mendonca (10)
All Saints Church In Wales Primary School, Llanedeyrn

Soaring High

Soaring high up to the sky,
Look back at Earth and say goodbye.
I go so high in the sky, I reach outer space,
I see alien creatures, and we all have a race.
Through the Milky Way and galaxies alike,
Faster and faster, like a dirt bike.

Soaring high up to the sky,
Look back at Earth and say goodbye.
Past planets, moons and the big ol' sun,
Oh, goody, goody, it's great, such fun.
The galaxy is vast, big and wide,
A small human like me would be lost inside,
Go so fast like a steam train spewing out steam,
The world is amazing, a Wonderverse dream.

Harriet Bulger (10)
Chichester Free School, Chichester

33

Summer Holidays

S targazing under the moonlit sky
U nder the stars, I shall lie
M y breath being taken over by the fireflies
M aking calming sounds as time goes by
E veryone sleeping as I sigh
R esting as I'm about to cry.

H olding a margarita as I tan by the pool
O n a sunbed keeping cool
L earning how to swim so I can win
I n the summer, at competitions
D uring the hot summer weather
A lways getting together
Y ay, it's begun
S ummer holidays.

Jovi Richardson (10)
Chichester Free School, Chichester

Emotions

E very day, I lie in bed,
M y thoughts and feelings fill my head.
O ver time, they start to grow,
T he odd emotion makes me question what I know.
I could cry for years and years,
O ver time I face my fears.
N ow I am as happy as can be,
S urrounded by joy, laughter and glee.

I hope you enjoyed reading my story,
Your life too can be filled with love and glory.
Letting your emotions free is the best thing
You can do, just trust me.

Olivia Pugsley (9)
Chichester Free School, Chichester

Friendship

F riendship is not a crime
R eading together with lots of rhyme
I n the class
E ndless hours pass of laugh, laugh, laugh
N ever hurt each other because that would end in disaster
D elighted about another player
S ky is blue, but we still do what we do
H ave lots of fun
I n the
P ark together.

Pia Pancheri (8)
Chichester Free School, Chichester

Where Will My Adventure Take Me Today?

Waking up, starting a new day,
Where will my adventure take me today?
I could be a superhero,
Or a builder making castles,
Defending my land,
And seeking out diamonds,
I could be a humble farming adventurer,
Roaming the land and making friends with a pig,
My imagination runs wild and free,
Creating a world, how I want it to be.

Lily Williams (9)
Chichester Free School, Chichester

The Axolotl

A xolotls are very cute
X ochimilco is the lake they live in
O r they get eaten
L ots in Japan
O h no! One lost a limb
T he axolotls can grow them back
L akes are their home.

Charlie Carter (8)

Chichester Free School, Chichester

Oh, Night Sky

Oh, night sky, are you alright?
Oh, night sky, don't you cry,
I hope you are alright tonight,
So don't worry.

So when the sun rises,
I won't forget you,
Oh, night sky.

Milton Arnell-Smith (10)
Chichester Free School, Chichester

Emotions

Emotions are happy and sad,
Emotions are excited and angry,
Emotions are ready and bored,
Emotions are calm and anxious,
Emotions are scared and relaxed,
Emotions are shame and hiding,
Emotions are kind and arrogant,
Emotions are brave and nervous,
Emotions are jealous and lonely,
Emotions are shocked and furious,
Emotions are frustrated and content,
Emotions are proud and ashamed,
Emotions are cruel and loving,
Emotions are dazed and confused,
Emotions are shy and confident,
Emotions are thrilled and exhausted
Emotions are tired and energetic,
Emotions are guilty and joyful,
Emotions are resistant and giving up
Emotions are cheerful and salty,
Emotions are happy and sad.

Dorothy Pughe (9)
Edmund Waller Primary School, London

The Mountain Of Emotions

How do I climb this mountain?
How do I reach the top?
With all these feelings weighing me down,
Quite the opposite of safe and sound.

Sad, happy, cross, unthinking,
Just the feeling of deep-down sinking.
Shivering, smiling, fake happy faces,
No answer for mysterious cases.

A boat sinking in a dark, cold sea,
A boat full of feelings, happiness is the key,
A mind full of sad, unforgettable thoughts,
Feelings, feelings that will never be caught.

The mountain is a hard, troublesome climb,
A climb that will soon get lost in time,
This is a poem of emotions and rhyme,
The poem of an unforgettable climb.

Sasja Macrory (9)
Edmund Waller Primary School, London

Nature

The wind blowing wildly,
The careful winter breeze flew on me.
Icicles as hard as crystals,
Break when they touch the soft ground.
The pond begins to freeze.
It glimmers in the moonlight,
As slippery as water.

The Christmas spirit comes to everybody,
Moving from house to house.
Everybody brings cheer and joy.
The sun sets,
As the sun goes down,
And the moon goes up.

It's the first of spring,
Flowers bloom,
And the bees buzz.
April's around the corner.

Easter comes,
And the Easter bunny,
Hides yummy chocolate,
In your house or gardens.

I come to watch nature in the woods,
And the birds chirp at me,
In a kind way.

Delilah Goulbourn (7)
Edmund Waller Primary School, London

Moonlight Owl

I look for you in the morning,
I look for you at noon,
I look for you before the rise of the moon.
But what is that sound?
I hear an owl. Great, dappled and bold.

And you sing for me by moonlight,
Watch for me by moonlight,
Stay with me by moonlight, till my night is done.

But you are not there in the day,
Sadly, softly, you float away.
But the day goes by and what do I hear?
An owl. Great, dappled and bold.

And you sing for me by moonlight,
Watch for me by moonlight,
Stay with me by moonlight,
But you won't be there in the day.

Elsie Chesterman (9)
Edmund Waller Primary School, London

Animals

Animals are wonderful,
Like pandas and possums.
Oh, how animals are wonderful,
Like monkeys and manatees.
Some are very mean, vicious or vile,
Others are kind, caring or cute.
The meanies are snakes, sharks and crocodiles.
It's not surprising how they all vary.
Some are wild, do tricks, or break records,
Some are humongous or even microscopic.
If you took a closer look,
You could see animals are all different shapes, sizes
and colours.
All animals have some beauty.
From tiny ants to enormous elephants,
Animals are wonderful.

Ben Connolly (7)
Edmund Waller Primary School, London

The Griffin

I have feathers as soft as a pillow,
My fur is like a cloud,
And when I open my beak,
My cry is very loud.

I soar above the mountaintops,
Searching for fuzzy sheep,
Their flesh I take, a bed I make
Out of the wool I keep.

My talons are razor-sharp daggers,
Perfect for eating a meal.
Because of my fur, wings, and feathers,
You know that I cannot be real.

Wren Hirst (9)
Edmund Waller Primary School, London

Animals

There are lots of animals in the world,
Exotic animals, urban animals,
Cute animals and tough animals,
There are lots of animals in the world.

There are lots of animals in the world,
Flying animals, walking animals,
Slow animals, fast animals,
And camouflaging animals,
There are lots of animals in the world.

Madeleine Spencer (8)
Edmund Waller Primary School, London

Animals

Animals, animals, animals, from mild parrots to lazy crocodiles
They always make you smile, some are fast, some are wacky,
Some are a bit fatty.
Some are deadly, some are wild,
And some are really mild.
We should not eat them but we should treat them
Like we really care and everyone loves them.

Sonny Ricketts (8)
Edmund Waller Primary School, London

In My Town There Are Lots Of Dogs

In my town, there are lots of dogs. There are big dogs, good dogs, spotty dogs, pitbulls, huskies, sausage dogs, golden Labs, black Labs, chocolate Labs, golden retrievers, pugs, tired dogs, different colour dogs, small dogs, big dogs, medium dogs, happy dogs, loving dogs, curious dogs, and lots more.

Rose Bomford (7)
Edmund Waller Primary School, London

Nature And The World

The ocean's deep blue seas,
With colourful coral,
Up to your knees.
Flooding with fishes,
Swimming from business.

The desert's rare green plants,
And its crunchy sand,
With its beautiful oasis,
Pumping life to all.

The clear blue skies,
Filled with fluffy white clouds,
Rain light down to Earth,
With all their glory.

While the forest's tall, towering trees,
Blast in the sky,
And on the ground,
The animals lie.
Silent in wait,
Stalking their prey.

Zac Wilcox (9)
Great Hollands Primary School, Bracknell

Spartan

First, we queued in the line,
But I needed the loo.
Then in we checked,
I saw a bird get pecked.
We got in and played tag,
It was fun, it was fab.
Then the team went to the loo,
I'm sure I heard someone shout moo.
Then we went to the start,
I smelled a fart.
Suddenly, we set off,
I could not help it; I needed to cough.
We went over walls,
At the top, a kid falls.
As we went in mud,
I almost lost my stud.
After two laps,
In the car, we all had naps.

Callan Rose (9)
Great Hollands Primary School, Bracknell

The Rainforest

R unning from the tribes in the rainforest
A heavy downpour from the clouds
I n a tribal house, the tip-tapping on the window
N o one is outside because of the heavy downpour
F ish are swimming in the stream
O h no, there's a hungry jaguar
R un, run, the jaguar's coming
E normous anaconda slithers up the canopy
S nakes slither on and look like vines
T oday I am hunting a jaguar as ferocious as a giant monster.

Caleb Pike (9)
Great Hollands Primary School, Bracknell

The Forests

I can hear a bear stomping its feet like a giant's heavy footsteps.
I can see fishes swimming in the lake.
I can hear birds tweeting in the trees.
I can see a deer chasing its friends.
I can smell a wet and soggy bird that has just got out of the water.
I can taste the crystal-clear waters of the frozen lake.
I can feel the plants' precious petals growing.
I can smell the pine needles from the trees.
Life in the forest is as calm as clouds floating on a sunny day.

Nevaeh Alleyne (9)
Great Hollands Primary School, Bracknell

Mountains

I heard there were mighty mechs, but they were deadly dragons.
I saw deadly, deep, dark caves as cramped as a box of chocolates.
I tasted the healing hot chocolate after the cold blizzards.
I touched the freezing, frozen, fizzling rivers, which were as creepy as a sneaky samurai.
I heard the whistling wind blowing blizzards, I smelled freezing food; I think they're as cold as an iceberg.

Cooper James (9)
Great Hollands Primary School, Bracknell

School

The school day starts at eight.
Oh no, it's history! I can't be late.
Happy children laughing and jumping.
Through the halls, so bright and thumping.

Oh yay! It's computing today!
We greet each other with a warm, "Hey"

Luckily, I really like my school.
I scored full marks on my test, twenty-five out of
twenty-five! So cool!

Nambung Rai (9)
Great Hollands Primary School, Bracknell

Fantastic Fortnite

F antastic Fortnite that I love to play
O utstanding active range that's in the obby
R ecreating references that I love
T racing trains to get good loot
N estling to snipe some players
I n this game, it's survival
T racking checkpoints to get some better loot
E very game bows down to this one.

Finnley Robinson (8)
Great Hollands Primary School, Bracknell

Poland

Food is a big key to Poland, the best cake in Poland is Sernik,
Sernik is as good as watching the sun set on the mountains,
Krakow is as fun as going on the fastest slide in the coral reef,
Boing, boing, there goes the rabbit across the field,
Caw, caw, caw, there goes the crow from the bird's nest,
Poland is a calm place in Europe.

Eryk Stepien (9)
Great Hollands Primary School, Bracknell

Roblox

I jump like a kangaroo
I type fast like a leopard running
My friend plays Roblox
She got hacked and she asked me for help.
In the escape room to solve the maths problem
But it was too hard, so I needed a rest.
I went to the obby and I tried to do it,
But it was too easy like doing a straddle.

Esme Rapy (9)
Great Hollands Primary School, Bracknell

Sense Poem

I can play with my rabbits.
I can hug my dogs.
I can stroke my cats.
I can hold my bearded dragon.
I can treat my tortoise.
I can watch my dogs play together.
I can pick up my rabbits.
I can sit with my cats.
I can take my dogs for a walk.
I love my animals and they love me.

Mia White (9)
Great Hollands Primary School, Bracknell

Angel

What is it?
It's as white as paper
It's as golden as a gold bar
It's as mythical as a dragon
It's as protective as a movie film
It's as incredible as a castle
But it's a... guardian angel.

Nitya Seechurn (8)
Great Hollands Primary School, Bracknell

What Is It?

It's as big as a tree.
It's as scary as a monster.
It's as mean as a bear.
It's as dangerous as a crocodile.
It's as cool as a museum.

Answer: It's a dragon alien.

Kaden Turner (8)
Great Hollands Primary School, Bracknell

What Is It?

It is as cold as Antarctica.
Has as much snow as winter in Greenland.
Lions roaring like cargo ships.
As beautiful as Niagara Falls.
Mountains towering over the land.
It's Narnia!

Arthur Higgs (8)
Great Hollands Primary School, Bracknell

Fantastic Fields

F lowers growing,

I nsects crawling,

E choes of the children playing,

L unches being eaten,

D ogs running and jumping,

S ilent thoughts in nature.

Jessica Hillsdon (9)

Great Hollands Primary School, Bracknell

Incoming

Can you hear me?
No answer.
Beep, beep, beep...
Silent whispers
Beep, beep, beep...
Is the ship abandoned?
Beep, beep, beep...
Hello, hello...
Beep, beep, beeeep.

Frankie Lewis (9)
Great Hollands Primary School, Bracknell

What Am I?

As short as a frog.
As scary as a bear.
As hard as a Mayan.
As long as string.
As fierce as a lion.
As tough as a tiger.

Answer: It's a crocodile.

Roman Smith-Chester (8)
Great Hollands Primary School, Bracknell

Guess

Children playing,
Classroom teaching,
Adults shouting,
Books slamming,
Pencil sharpening,
Projectors displaying,
Did you guess?
It was school.

Florence Payne (8)
Great Hollands Primary School, Bracknell

What Is It?

It's as giant as a house.
It's as scary as a ghost.
It's as sharp as spikes.
It's as dangerous as a hammer.
It is a dinosaur.

Hang Wong (8)
Great Hollands Primary School, Bracknell

Riddle

It is as small as a crab,
It is as painful as a cactus.
It's as black as the midnight sky,
It is as fast as a lizard.
It is a scorpion.

Layla Mullins (9)
Great Hollands Primary School, Bracknell

Minecraft

Mines are a dangerous place
As dangerous as the Nether
Powerful as a warden
As powerful as TNT explosions
I can smell lava chickens.

Luke Murphy (9)
Great Hollands Primary School, Bracknell

Cinema

It is as fun as a museum,
It is a fun place,
You eat popcorn,
You drink fizzy drinks.
Did you guess it?
It is the cinema.

Scarlett Morgan (9)
Great Hollands Primary School, Bracknell

Aliens And Jeff (Part One)

It was a normal day for Jeff
Tea and biscuits, oh, please, yes!
But then, shining through the window
Circle-shaped ominous shadows
Here, Jeff was freaking out!
Uh oh! Aliens screamed and shouted!
Suddenly, off he flew past the moon
A great view of the Earth, he once knew
Mars, Jupiter, or Saturn? Who'd have known?
There's so much in space, so let's go!
Landing on an alien planet
I wondered what was happening with my friend Janet.
I was escorted to this fancy lab
Where they did experiments on humans. It was not so fab!
I met my best friend, Bob
He was missing for a while, so I was glad he wasn't gone
I learnt that this place was called Zon
But all I knew was that I wanted to go back home.

Max E (11)
Hartsfield JMI Primary School, Baldock

The Eternal Seasons

Spring, dew lies on the ground
Spring, pollen whips through the winds
Spring, lambs and bunnies run through the fields
Spring, flowers sit in a bed.

Summer, the sun makes days last forever
Summer, ice cream drips onto the ground
Summer, bees and wasps whoosh around
Summer, long-lasting holidays all across the world.

Autumn, golden brown leaves dance on the ground
Autumn, people dress up in zombie and vampire costumes
Autumn, schools pile people with work
Autumn, hedgehogs and foxes run in the darkness.

Winter, trees get decorated with lights and baubles
Winter, fireworks go off as people celebrate the New Year
Winter, turkey and potatoes fill tables
Winter, animals hibernate in the woods.

Lottie R (11)
Hartsfield JMI Primary School, Baldock

Lion's Roar

Eyes like a flaming ball of fire.
Jumps onto his prey like he's never been tired.

Leaps onto rocks with no fear on his face.
Animals are hiding from disgrace.

The lion is proud – never been prouder.
If you get even close, it will turn you into powder.

Even a touch will rip your core.
Then he will pierce your ears with an ear-splitting roar.

At the end of the day, it has a sleep.
Not letting out even the smallest weep.

In the morning, the cycle starts again,
Jumping on prey like he's never been tired.
But really, all he wants to do is lie and be quiet.

Betsy Fletcher (11)
Hartsfield JMI Primary School, Baldock

The Seasons

Ice cream, sun, sand and sea
This really is the place to be
Laughter, fun, friends and glee
Blossom falling from the trees.

But summer doesn't last forever,
Autumn comes, and so does the cold weather
Comforting home and sweets galore
Halloween has returned once more.

Every day, getting colder and colder
Christmas is coming closer and closer
Tinsel wrapped around the tree
Cinnamon smell fills the air.

Tulips rising from the earth,
Newborn animals, lambs and piglets.

All the seasons. What's your favourite?

Milly Reynolds (11)
Hartsfield JMI Primary School, Baldock

The Band

A group of people with drums and a mic,
Let's make a song about taking flight.
We need to pick a genre, so many to choose,
I know! Let's do blues.
We need a name for our album,
Choose some song names and compare them.
Doing this stuff is such a pleasure,
I know! Call the album Treasure.
We need to do a concert in the town,
I just hope we don't go down.
Oh look, we're making millions,
Maybe we can make it billions.
Now we are the best in the world,
I just hope it won't take loads.

Adam Fixter (10)
Hartsfield JMI Primary School, Baldock

Bug In A Mug

B ug in a mug.
U p above the rug.
G ot a name, that was Doug.

I n the mug there was a bug.
N ext to the bug in a rug lived the other bug, the one in the mug.

A nd soon a few bugs moved like the one in the rug.

M ug soon got filled with the bug's babies, only a few.
U p above the rug lived another bug, the one in the mug.
G ot killed when somebody filled the mug with boiling water and so gave his family one last hug.

Max R (11)
Hartsfield JMI Primary School, Baldock

The War Of The Broken

A foggy morning, the hope all dead

Back on the battlefield, not here again
People's heads bowed, in a shield of solitude
The other countries attacking, rather rude

Not seeing families for months and months on end,
Loneliness creeps over
Snow falls down like no other, oh no, it's getting colder
Gunshots trigger their fragile selves, this is getting scary,
Oh, why me, why me?

Annabelle White (11)
Hartsfield JMI Primary School, Baldock

Baked Beans

B aked beans in their can
E asy to sizzle in a pan
A fter sizzling, serve with cheese
N ever ever forget to say please
S ome may hate beans, but I do not.

L oving them is my life
O h, those beans so saucy and nice
V ery tasty, sometimes with rice
E at those beans, guzzle 'em down
R eally nice, go to town.

Luna Constantinou (11)
Hartsfield JMI Primary School, Baldock

A Crab's Life

Crabs, oh crabs,
With their claws.
Oh so sad,
When dipped in sauce.
Scuttle around the beach all day,
Until they finally hit the hay.

Always swimming in the sea,
Hopefully not served with peas.
Do not give them to a fisherman,
Or sizzle them in a pan.
Or eat them with a slice of ham.
If you ever meet a crab,
You will see they are so fab

Beth Sutton (11)
Hartsfield JMI Primary School, Baldock

The Bunny And The Frog

As the first of the autumn leaves fell,
A small, young bunny walked up to a well
Made of a short, hollowed-out log,
He peered inside and saw a dark green frog.

Picking it up, the bunny tried to help,
But as soon as he touched it, the frog started to yelp.
The small, young bunny dropped it back in the well,
And ran away from where the autumn leaves fell.

Arthur Keay (11)
Hartsfield JMI Primary School, Baldock

You Have A Choice

Light and Dark, two brothers of hate and love,
Two opposites, one more caring and one more weirdly fun,
Light loved his beloved mum,
While Dark drank bottles of rum,
Still having much more dangerous fun.
Dark told lies when Light spoke truth,
This is a poem, where you can choose,
Will you be Light, and speak right?
Or be Dark and live a daring life?

Cyril (11)
Hartsfield JMI Primary School, Baldock

The Ballerina

As she prances through the night,
Her eyes so sparkly bright.
On the midnight show,
She wears a pastel pink bow.

With her dress so fine,
She holds her line.
She dances through dreams,
So light and dutiful,
Her presence is so beautiful.

Will it end?
Well I wish it wouldn't,
This ballerina,
Stole the show.

Olivia Raheja (11)
Hartsfield JMI Primary School, Baldock

The Shark Who Likes McDonald's

Sharky, sharky
As big as a mountain
And when he comes, be prepared
As his favourite food is McDonald's!
Yes, it's true!
Does he want a cheeseburger?
Or a double cheeseburger?
A triple cheeseburger?
No!
He wants an infinite cheeseburger.
The very next day, he decided to become a planet as he was as big as a big bum!

William Cartwright (10)
Hartsfield JMI Primary School, Baldock

Cosmic Spaghetti

Sweet and spicy sauce,
Soaring through the multiverse.
The noodles stretch like a cosmic maze,
Slowly sliding like a worm,
Through the giant abyss.

Spicy meatballs burn your tongue,
Like the burning sun.
A universe of taste,
Where stars and spice align.
Across the cosmic tapestry,
Flavours intertwine.

Marley Banks (10)
Hartsfield JMI Primary School, Baldock

The Swordsman

The swordsman whom you've never met,
He spins and parries in a fight,
He brings terror to those he has fougnt,
He can stand a chance against any foe,
Even one wielding a powerful bow.

You will know when he comes,
Wielding two lordy long swords,
He will always come on a full moon,
Beware of the swordsman.

Oscar Richards (11)
Hartsfield JMI Primary School, Baldock

Football's Coming Home

F ootball's coming home today

O h no! We're down

O h yes! We are back again

T wo, one! Two, one!

B ellingham runs down the wing

A whistle blows for half-time

L ucky us, we're in the lead

L et's hope we don't bottle it this time.

Leo M (11)
Hartsfield JMI Primary School, Baldock

Fire

Fire, fire,
Flicker and flow,
Flying through the wood.

Like a hot oven,
Orange and red,
Crackling through the forest.

Hot and bothered,
Fire is mean,
When we are cold, it's a saviour.

Flaming hot,
The sun shall burn us,
Giving us light for the dark.

Harry M (11)
Hartsfield JMI Primary School, Baldock

?

It glowed with an otherworldly light.
No one knew what was on the other side.
Could be anything, I guess.
The edge of space, flying pigs!
But no one knew.
They could only guess.
It just lay there,
Waiting for someone,
For their curiosity to tip over
For someone to find out.

Sam Vall (11)
Hartsfield JMI Primary School, Baldock

Summertime

Summer, how nice the fresh air feels.
Summer, taking a step on the beach,
The warm golden sand under your feet.
Summer, the salty sea breeze.

Summer, the cold, refreshing
Sea water under your feet.
Summer, can you feel the sun shining
On your back as you paddle in the sea?

Lacie Waldock (11)
Hartsfield JMI Primary School, Baldock

Football

F ans like to watch teams play
O f course, I train in the garden
O f course, it is the best sport ever
T he match is exciting
B all boys should be respected
A ll people can play it
L overs of the game
L ove and respect everyone.

Harrison Parker (10)
Hartsfield JMI Primary School, Baldock

Harry Potter

Harry Potter's life,
So much hatred and sorrow.
Lily and James Potter loved Harry so,
They gave up their life fighting bold Voldemort.
But later on, Harry went through some trouble,
Fighting Voldemort about five to six times,
And meeting some loved ones along the way.

Martha (11)
Hartsfield JMI Primary School, Baldock

Mmm, Cheese Toasties

Cheese toasties are better than cake
If you disagree, you've made a mistake
I have them at night, in the morning they're nice
I eat them all over the place
I have them on my bike and when I eat my rice
I couldn't do without them
Cheese toasties are my life!

Sadie Evans (11)
Hartsfield JMI Primary School, Baldock

Sesame Street

E very red person walking down the street is

L ike me - cool and sneaky!

M ost red people just walk down the street and don't even take a glance at me.

O ver there is me! Yes, that's right - I'm Elmo, taking a stroll down Sesame Street!

Eli Kendall (11)

Hartsfield JMI Primary School, Baldock

Butterfly

Butterfly
When I fly so high
A twinkling glitter falls beneath my feet.

Butterfly
Colours going left and right
And even twirling around and around.

Butterfly
As I twirl and twirl in the sky
Almost making me dizzy.

Lily-Mae Furse (11)
Hartsfield JMI Primary School, Baldock

Winter!

W oolly hats and windy days.
I ndoors is where the heat stays.
N ever not shivering.
T ime to have some fun in the snow!
E ven though it's always cold...
R emember it only comes once a year.

Isabel (11)
Hartsfield JMI Primary School, Baldock

Winter

W inter is when snow falls
  I cicles point like stalactites
  N o leaves remain on trees
  T he days grow ever shorter
  E ach person decorating a tree
  R acks of firewood in every home.

Bradley (11)
Hartsfield JMI Primary School, Baldock

The Lone Wolf

The wolf stood alone
Except for his bone
At the moon he howls
And in the night he prowls
His eyes, dark like the void
Jaws impossible to avoid
In the grass he lay
Ready to strike his prey.

Barnaby Reid (11)
Hartsfield JMI Primary School, Baldock

Oh, How I Love You

The sun is shining,
Just like you,
Oh, how I love you.

I wake up
To see you,
Oh, how I love you.

I had a dream,
Can't you see?
Oh, how I love you.

Labella McCarthy (11)
Hartsfield JMI Primary School, Baldock

My Pirate Ship

As I float around on
My pirate ship a cannon blasts
Into my ears like a tornado
On the tip of
My ship as I eat one piece
Of my meat,
I scream, "I am *king!*"

Rex Willett (11)
Hartsfield JMI Primary School, Baldock

Phoenix

P ork eater
H eir of the birds
O rder keeper
E mpire of the flames
N ice bird
I gnited bird,
X ylophone burner.

Harry H (11)
Hartsfield JMI Primary School, Baldock

What Am I?

I'm full of water,
With lots of sand,
Shells lie on the ground,
What am I?

Answer: I am the beach.

Lottie Haden (11)
Hartsfield JMI Primary School, Baldock

Dragons

Fire breather
Gold hoarder
Treasure stealer
Day sleeper
Scale cleaner
Blood spiller.

Joni Martin (11)
Hartsfield JMI Primary School, Baldock

The Kitty Cat

C utie
A s fluffy as fur
T he purr of a lifetime
S uper cool.

Alexander DT (10)

Hartsfield JMI Primary School, Baldock

Imaginary Galaxy

I t's a place everyone wants to see.

M agical streaks of pink, purple and blue flood the air.

A s beautiful and sparkly as the sea.

G azing

I nto the distance.

N ever-ending night sky void.

A mazed and thoughtful, you're standing still in a trance.

R emembering behind you is something so big.

Y ew trees and planets spinning away.

G reat stars all around you.

A sight you cannot miss.

L ovely and cosy is what you will see.

A ll you can see is a dream come true.

X ylophones and pianos are heard ahead too

Y ou've loved it here, so no doubt soon you'll close your eyes again and imagine a place like this and make it come true.

Zaynab Shah (10)
Kennington Primary School, Fulwood

Sometimes I Wish I Were In Space

Sometimes, I wish I were in space,
Floating in my spacesuit, miles and miles away.

Sitting in the ISS, out of all the astronauts, I will be the best.
All the way from 1969, my trip will be a great success.

Jumping across Mercury, Venus, Mars,
I will then rest and gaze upon the stars.

Dancing around Jupiter, Saturn, Uranus, Neptune,
I will then collect upon the moon.

Sometimes, I wish I were in space,
Jumping across galaxies without a trace.

Now all I know has been forgotten,
I can't remember what I've learned,
Oh well, it's time to go back to Earth.

When I get back, I will be known as the great astronaut,
Inayah Qazi, the one who defied all laws of gravity.

Inayah Qazi (10)
Kennington Primary School, Fulwood

Oh Summer's England

Oh, summer's England, the time has come
The sun is high, the joy has sprung.
Families gather for barbecue delight,
Laughter and chatter stretch into the night.

The grass is trimmed, the ball rolls free,
Football with friends, wild and carefree.
To the beach we go, with a big bright smile,
Hoping the sunshine stays awhile.

Ice cream melts in eager hands,
Footprints trail across the sands.
The warmth beneath my feet feels right,
Golden grains glowing in the light.

A butterfly lands on my nose, then flies –
Its wings like petals in the skies.
The air is fresh with ocean's song,
I wish these sunny days stayed long.

Zayn Sheth (10)
Kennington Primary School, Fulwood

Europe

Europe is a great place to enjoy and live,
So there is a lot of credit you need to give.

London, Madrid, Milan and Berlin,
And make sure you put rubbish in the bin.

Waffles, gelato, pizza and chips,
Let's go to Blackpool for a trip.

Lots of competitions are happening,
So many fans are chanting and singing.

Scotland, Sweden, Germany and Denmark,
England has a lot of parks.

The sun is shining on my face,
While kids are having a quick race.

If I could've, I would've taken pictures,
If you go to Europe, there are a lot of adventures.

Muhammad Amin Bhura (10)
Kennington Primary School, Fulwood

Glorious Nature

I wish I were nature's friend,
Dancing around the flowers,
Climbing trees for hours.
I'd go around the bushes,
Picking berries as I go.

I wish I were nature's friend,
Who was always by their side,
I'd pick all the flowers,
Waving them around.
I'd run around the gardens,
Until I couldn't anymore.

I just wish I were nature,
Then I wouldn't have to
Worry about anything.

Safiyyah Alam (10)
Kennington Primary School, Fulwood

Antarctica

Calm landscape, like a fake statue,
Beautiful ocean, like people in this world,
Ice landscape, like someone falling off a slide,
Waddling penguins, like ticking clocks,
Icebergs shifting and drifting apart, like heartbreak,
Light blue sky, like a calm ocean,
People in the distance looking very cold, like they're
about to be a statue,
Cold sea being powerful, like an earthquake,
The sky being white, like cotton candy.

Aizah Khalid (10)
Kennington Primary School, Fulwood

The Wonder Of Space

Sometimes when I stare into the sky, I wonder what it feels like to have something in the sky,
So come with me and we will explore all the wonders of the system.

As we launch, we say goodbye for adventure.
As we land, we'll pray to God that we survive.
Mercury, Venus, Mars, Jupiter, Saturn, Neptune, Uranus,
And don't forget sad little Pluto.
Now it's time to say goodbye.

Ali Ayub (10)
Kennington Primary School, Fulwood

My Magical Land

Who, what, where?
I am in a magical land,
I feel electrified from my toes to my hair.
I can see moonlit stars in the sky like sand.

Dragons hiss,
Horses leap,
Phoenixes breathe.

One,
Two,
Three,
Wow, this is my...
Magical land!
Electrified birds,
Water dragons,
Air monks,
This is
My magical land.

Mustafa Ayub (10)
Kennington Primary School, Fulwood

Dog Man

The
Big, black
Sky took over the
Night as powerful Petey
Started striking. Houses burned
As people sighed sadly and cried
Then came the dangerous Dog Man
Bringing back the large light
As the people cheerfully
Cheered, and as
Petey passed
Out
Dog Man
Had won and
Periless Petey had
Of course
Lost!

Mohammed Hassan Shaikh (9)
Kennington Primary School, Fulwood

Antarctica

The sea,
As bouncy as a dolphin,
Up and down.
The ice pack shattered,
Like shattered glass.

The ice shelf,
Stays up like a fortress,
That would never give up.
The ice,
Is as cold as a fridge.
The sea,
Is as cold as a bucket of ice.

Naad-e-Ali Kazmi (10)
Kennington Primary School, Fulwood

Space Or School?

Space, space, space, oh
A wonderful place.

School is school, school,
Oh why can't we rule?

A horrendous place
In school or space.

Space or school?
In school or space.

I think school,
Because adults
Rule!

Ayesha Bargit (9)
Kennington Primary School, Fulwood

A Very Big Carrot Lover

White, fluffy marshmallows,
All over the floor,
They look like little pillows
That melt my heart to the core.

I walk into the room,
All the attention goes to me,
When I see something fluffy,
I just want to keep one, please!

What am I?

Zahraa Harif (9)
Kennington Primary School, Fulwood

The Four Seasons

Spring,
Summer,
Autumn,
Winter,
They're all great,
But which one is truly the best?
Spring bursting with flowers,
Summer shining in the sun,
Autumn covering up the land with crunchy leaves
And winter sprinkling the atmosphere with snow.

Zeyad Patel (10)
Kennington Primary School, Fulwood

Space!

Look at the night skies
To see what lies
There are eight planets
And don't worry, there is enough
Time to learn it!
Mercury, Venus
Earth, Mars
Jupiter, Saturn
Uranus, Neptune!
We can't forget...
The moon and Pluto!

Rumaisah Matki (10)
Kennington Primary School, Fulwood

Why Antarctica Is A Dangerous Place

The size of an elephant, the breaking ice can end your life.
Towering like skyscrapers, the glaciers looked over the Endurance.
The glaciers reached skyward, like icy versions of the Burj Khalifa.
The orcas swim freely – for now!

Isa Pepi (10)
Kennington Primary School, Fulwood

Nature Is Everywhere

Nature is everywhere,
Everywhere in the air.
Snakes are sly,
While butterflies fly.
Leaves drip with water,
From clouds sky high.
Nature is everywhere,
Everywhere in the air.

Isa Wadee (10)
Kennington Primary School, Fulwood

The Lost Astronaut

Lost in sight
Full of fright
Drifting in the night
Gazing at the starlight
Light doesn't live here...
Only you do, my friend...
Or should I say...
The lost astronaut...

San Rassul (10)
Kennington Primary School, Fulwood

Anglo-Saxon's Swords

Flat blades,
War bringer,
Blood spiller,
Precious swords,
People protector,
Prestigious weapon,
Treasure seeker,
Battle winner.

Zidan Khandia (10)
Kennington Primary School, Fulwood

The Park

Tree shaker,
Wind maker,
Bird feeder,
Fun bringer,
Bird singer,
Slippery slide,
Pond maker,
Tree grower,
Island builder.

Samuel Hamilton-Gray (9)
Kennington Primary School, Fulwood

Nature

Wind blower,
Leaf rustler,
Tree grower,
Life taker,
Sight seer,
Death bringer.

Amina Hussain (9)
Kennington Primary School, Fulwood

Miss Bottom

There was a very strict teacher,
She was more like a preacher,
All the children were scared.
Her name was Miss Bottom,
She was horrible and rotten.
She had a very long nose,
And a wart on her big toe.

Joe was five minutes late.
"Sorry, Miss," said Joe.
"Sorry is not good enough!
Go to another classroom,
Be gone!"
And just like that,
Joe disappeared.

"I am Miss Bottom,
And you will all obey!"
Rex giggled with glee,
Then all of a sudden,
She turned Rex into a pea.
"Who else wants to disobey?"
Not me,
No way!

The day dragged,
And we were stuck in,
With wet play.
Could this day get any worse?
We felt like we were cursed.
"Can I have some water please, Miss?"
"No," replied Miss Bottom,
"You can die of thirst!"

Hometime finally came,
Where we were free.
"Let's run to Mum.
Oh no! I forgot my lunchbox."
I went back to the classroom,
Where I saw Miss Bottom,
Fly off on her broom.

Tiffany Monford (10)
Linton Mead Primary School, Thamesmead

The Shop Of Ancient Wonders

You will hear a *creak* coming from up high,
A book of glow left its secrets behind,
You can learn from its force,
How to turn people into gold, of course.

My magic shop has intricate windows,
That will award you the view of the shimmering,
moonlit sky.
They purely have no limits for feasting your eyes.
If you come and look at the majestic butterfly,
It won't only flutter, it will shatter, and turn to butter.

The greatest magic you will see,
Is from the deceiving toffees,
Fantastically, they will make you spill
Your biggest secrets.
On the top bookshelf lie books,
That have hurricanes shifting through them.

Step in wonder, the magic is alive,
Take a peek at my magic shop,
It will bring pixie dust to your mind.
This shop will make you the most wondrous version
Of yourself there will ever be,
Are *you* going to enter the shop beyond limits?

Elizaveta Nikulina (10)
Linton Mead Primary School, Thamesmead

Always There For You

Look around you
As you can see
There are so many people
You can be!
From idols to rescuers
It never ends
Though you chose to be
Where you are
Even with so many
Ideas and possibilities
Sometimes you let go of these dreams
Which saddens you
But don't worry
We'll be there for you!
All you need is hope and shimmers
Shining through the air while you giggle!
And some things can be hard to push through
But with an ember ingrained in your heart
No one can stop you!
And trust me
It really is the truth.

Daena Julia Castro (10)
Linton Mead Primary School, Thamesmead

The Making Of Magic

In the mystical lands
Everything that could ever be dreamt of came true
Pixies, unicorns, phoenixes, wisps whispering secrets
and even dragons
Some things that came in the night
And some things that came in the light.

Mellow vibes flowing in the air
Doughnuts were growing on trees, ripe for the plucking
High in the sky were rain clouds full of hopes and
dreams
Cupcakes shooting out of the ground like mushrooms.

A magical place up in the sky
A mystical place, so very high
Come if you want to see your dream come true.

Imogen Mulheran (10)
Linton Mead Primary School, Thamesmead

The Magical Shop

In my shop, I shall put candyfloss clouds, raining lollipops, an edible ice cream sculpture as tasty as tiramisu, a flaming phoenix as bright as the sun, a waterfall of chocolate vanilla
In my shop, I shall put magical books as tall as the roof, a cursed armoury as evil as darkness, a magical telephone that opens the door when it rings, a unicorn's heart wrapped in a dove's feathers.
My shop, it has the smoothest doors right now, but the darkest secret back then,
My shop, catch us (out of the air) before we vanish.

Rayan Mesbah (9)
Linton Mead Primary School, Thamesmead

Poems, Poets

This is a poem
Just like any other
But there's a twist
Poems, poets
Poet is somebody
That plans, drafts, and
Publishes poems
It really is quite impressive
But to be fair
If you try hard enough
You can be one too!

This is a poem
Just like any other
But there's a twist
Poems, poets
Poet is somebody
Like any other
But they have a job
To whisk the reader
Into a magical story.

Henry Sadagos (10)
Linton Mead Primary School, Thamesmead

The Twenty Animals (Vet)

In my vet, I shall put
A cat that is wearing a green hat,
A bat that has a mat,
A fox that can box,
And a fish that can kiss.

In my shop, I shall put
A snake with a cake,
A tiger that is a liar,
A toad crossing the road,
And a bird with a nerd.

My shop has the most oldest dogs and old animals,
They are all interesting.

Maleeah Grima (9)
Linton Mead Primary School, Thamesmead

My Favourite Food Is Sushi

M y second favourite food is noodles, they are squiggly and long.
Y ou don't like sushi? That is totally wrong!

F or Rayan, my brother, I would roll him a fishy delight.
A t dinner we munch it, from noon until night.
V ery wiggly seaweed wrapped up so tight.
O ver my head I dream of sushi at night.
U nder my bed I once found a sushi roll.
R eal or pretend? I don't know.
I ate it anyway, please don't tell Mum.
T asted a bit like fish-flavoured gum.
E ven the cat wanted some.

F ishy and fun, it's my number one dish.
O ne bite of sushi and I make a wish.
O n my birthday, I'll eat a whole tray.
D on't steal my sushi or I'll run away.

Aliyah Hatab (9)
Rosetta Primary School, London

Wonderverse

W hat an awesome competition with a prize of £100!

O range is the colour of anxiety. Don't need to fear, they are always here!

N ever-ending stress, just take a breath.

D etermined girl named Lana making a poem for Wonderverse.

E verlasting hope, begging for the prize!

R are poem you can't find anywhere.

V elvet red handwriting pen running across the paper.

E nding the competition is sad, but I loved the opportunity!

R acing cars soaring through my brain like Lightning McQueen!

S ometimes I lose, but that is okay.

E xciting memories are being made.

Lana Tahmim (8)
Rosetta Primary School, London

Better Together

B etter together? Oh, it's all true.
E very day, being together, no matter what.
T he tremendous bond we all have,
T ime passes by, but we all stay.
E ven though we are different, we can still be kind,
R esilient to stay together, no matter what.

T ogether is the path to friendship,
O n the moon, or even here.
G ive it a try and you'll see,
E ven if you don't want to.
T he feeling spreads in your heart,
H e or she, it doesn't matter,
E veryone is unique and that's okay,
R emember to stay together.

Afnan Arifi (9)
Rosetta Primary School, London

Friendship

Friendship is all about trust,
Believing someone will be kind and honest,
Sticking by someone's side,
No matter what kind.
Always be caring and thoughtful,
Light, happy, laughter shared with a friend.

Let me tell you all about bonds.
A bond is a strong connection between people.
Supporting is the best thing,
It means helping someone when they need it.
Always forgive people,
Let go of hurt after someone says sorry.

If you're not alone, share time or experiments,
Treat each other in a fair and caring way.
You need to understand,
And know how someone feels.

Zara Munsha (9)
Rosetta Primary School, London

Flying Man

Flying man, flying man, how high do you fly?
Up and above the observable sky.
Flying and free as an endangered beautiful butterfly
Swear I saw a dancing hero through the sky.

The clouds moved aside, making a pathway as long as
Hadrian's Wall
Sunlight played on his shoulder like a giant fireball
As he flies with the wind surrounding him
Also takes care of us by putting ocean rubbish in bins.

I dream of flying with the flying man in Japan
Going on an adventure through Milan
Dear flying man, can you please take me to Legoland?

Haider Ali Asad (9)
Rosetta Primary School, London

Sunshine

S unshine makes everyone bloom with happiness.

U nder the journey to ancient Greece the sun appears with boiling power.

N o fear, just braveness. Has more adventures than anyone on the planet.

S o challenging and wise with power that no one has.

H opeful wishes come true when the sun changes to the moon.

I ce melts when the sun roars, with sandy hot air the water flies.

N o one can defeat the hot ball of fire.

E verything it does, graceful and kind, makes the planet happier.

Alicja Borzecka (8)
Rosetta Primary School, London

Gymnastics

G reat time and time for finale,

Y et hard, but gymnasts are flexible.

M aybe not that flexible, but flexible enough for first place!

N ever perfect, always makes mistakes,

A lways trying hard to get every bit right!

S how your best skills,

T uck jump, get your knees to your chest!

I n here, do not make a mistake on purpose.

C artwheel really good, they have to point their toes.

S traddle-jump as high as you can, straighten your legs!

Ieva Kalinauskaite (9)

Rosetta Primary School, London

Friendship

F riendship is a close group of friends that is never broken.

R un to your friends, help them if they need help,

I n the park, friends play happily,

E veryone loves their friends and cares for them,

N ever break a promise,

D on't leave your friendship,

S tay together happily,

H aving fun with your lovely friends,

I n your heart, love your friends with all your heart,

P eople care about you like how you care about your friends.

Fedora Naniwono (9)
Rosetta Primary School, London

Football

F ernandes plays extremely well for Manchester United

O nana plays in the position of goalkeeper for Manchester United

Ø degaard plays for Arsenal as a midfielder

T imber played well for Arsenal in the Champions League

B ellingham is a British person

A nd he plays for Real Madrid, my favourite team

L ampard played for England, but he is now retired

L ewis-Skelly plays for Arsenal in the left back and takes most of the outs.

Ziad Haidari (9)
Rosetta Primary School, London

Friendship

F riendship is all we need.

R eally, that's all we need.

I love my friends to the moon and back.

E ven though they aren't family.

N ever reject your friends.

D on't even if they have a fight with friends.

S o play with them and don't fight.

H eaven is just like your friends.

I enjoy playing, and I'm sure you do too.

P eacefully playing and talking with them.

Nana Aba Dzigbodi (9)

Rosetta Primary School, London

Spider-Man

S ticky webs hang on walls
P eople love Spider-Man
I n his heart, he is powerful and fearless
D angerous, but saving people's lives
E normously brave and a role model to everyone
R esilient and famous, will always be safe.

M indful, hopeful and a kind-hearted person
A lways celebrates his victories from battles
N ever gives up and is a true hero.

Sreyansh Aryal (8)
Rosetta Primary School, London

Paradise

P aradise, that's where a lot of good people will go,

A lso, you'll get anything you want, I know,

R iding super cool cars, having the best time of your life,

A t the free mansion, eating lots of food,

D oing all your favourite things,

I 'm sure you'll have the best time of your life,

S ee all the pretty birds singing,

E verything is perfect there.

Arissa Ahmed (9)
Rosetta Primary School, London

Avayah

A vayah is smart, has lots of knowledge.
V ery pretty, has curly hair as brown as a bear.
A nimals are my best friend, but so is Maddison.
Y ou need a friend. *Boom!* I am here for playtime.
A s I spread youthful spirits everywhere.
H ope you enjoy my poem. Happy, joyful, jump
everywhere, I look everywhere, I am everywhere!

Avayah Pierre (9)
Rosetta Primary School, London

Memories

M emories are the best thing on my mind.

E motions are always getting better.

M ore love and support.

O ut in the world with your friends.

R emember those old memories.

I think they are the thing that keeps me alive.

E njoy it while you survive.

S eason by season those old memories, they never die.

Lara Zenti (9)

Rosetta Primary School, London

Space

S ilence all over the pitch-black sky of forever night,
P itch-black frozen air as you glide through the
weightless forever night,
A cold mist blazing through your body, but really in
your mind, are still cosmic vibes,
C olourful stars all around your space body,
E nd of the universe, unfortunately, not a thing.

Mateo Hernandez (8)
Rosetta Primary School, London

Joyful

J oy bursts into me every single day.

O ver joy always hits my heart, and i feel joy no matter what.

Y our day could feel better when you see sunshine, which is as bright as the sunshine

F or the cure of sadness, joy will always be the cure.

U nbelievably, happiness makes joy.

L et everyone be joyful.

Amaya Sahni (9)
Rosetta Primary School, London

Friendship

F riends keep me happy
R eal friends are honest
I n the house, we eat rice
E very one of them is nice
N ever scatter the group
D ecent behaviour they do
S unflowers are nice
H ealthy kids eat rice
I n the house, we play
P lay games all day.

Marsad Mohammed (8)
Rosetta Primary School, London

Imagination

I t is a magical world
M aybe it can be even more amazing
A world of wonder
G reater than ever
I n an amazing world
N o world can be better
A magical world
T ea is amazing
I t is wonderful
O n this world
N o galaxy is better.

Zaid Shariff (9)

Rosetta Primary School, London

Sprunki

S prunki is a very fun game,
P ut and drag the icons to the polo.
R eady to make some fun music?
U pbeat all the time,
N ow time for fun, let's go to the horror mode!
K illing most of the sprunkies, don't be scared,
I t will be fun, go try it now!

Reynaldo Augustine Gatchalian (8)
Rosetta Primary School, London

Happy

H elp others so you can smile at others and be happy.

A gift a day keeps the sorrow away.

P eople will help you become happy if you help them.

P ick people who will help you.

Y ou are happy, don't think of sorrow. Try to think of happy and talk to someone.

Kevin Chen (9)
Rosetta Primary School, London

School

S chool can sometimes be annoying,
C ould sometimes be fun, or not
H owever, it's good for your education,
O r it's good for fitness like PE,
O r there might be strict rules, which are hard.
L eaving can be sad, but it might be for a reason.

Rayan Dohlal (9)
Rosetta Primary School, London

West Ham

W hy don't we have fun?
E very choice could mean life or death,
S hining bright like a diamond,
T ogether, we embrace light.

H ope rises with the dawn,
A dventure calls. Don't be the same,
M ake wishes soar and gleam.

Azhaan Chowdhury (9)
Rosetta Primary School, London

Seasons

S easons are three months long a year,
E veryone was born in a season,
A n example is summer, that is June,
S o many months for the season,
O ctober is in autumn,
N ovember is the end of fall,
S pring, summer, autumn and winter!

Evie Bonnett (8)

Rosetta Primary School, London

Nature

N ature is nice and ancient,
A nd nature, like the blue, small and tiny raindrops,
T he things are very relaxing and calm,
U p in the trees, birds chirping and enormous trees,
R eally relaxing, nice and silent,
E arly days, birds singing.

Adeeb Rahman (9)
Rosetta Primary School, London

Forest

F rom the trees to the monkeys,
O n the ground floor, where the lions are,
R esting, as all the birds are chirping,
E asy for the bugs but hard for animals,
S winging as goldfish swim across rivers,
T iming chases for big, scary prey.

Adam Kessira (9)
Rosetta Primary School, London

Summer

S ummer is hot while the sun is shining

U sing a pool to cool down

M elting hot, but playing around

M easles, hotter than the sun right now

E ating ice cream, yum, yum, yum

R ight now, having fun in the burning hot sun.

Mila Saber (9)

Rosetta Primary School, London

Spring

S pring is the best season.
P retty blossoms smell beautiful because of spring.
R eally, spring is the best!
I wish we had spring forever!
N ever leave me, spring!
G uess spring is gonna stay with me forever.

Alexandra Tiganescu (9)
Rosetta Primary School, London

Spring

S unlight pours towards the ground
P etals reach to the sky
R abbits run across the blooming meadow
I nsects wake up from their slumber
N ew beginnings
G rateful for new chances in life.

An Gia Nguyen (9)

Rosetta Primary School, London

Mindful

Awesome adventures
Happen every day.
Helpful friends
Make the world a better place.

Polite care
Shows us words for others.
Young joy
Is full of hearts and fun.
Playful minds
Have the best ideas.

Cristhofer Pachon (9)
Rosetta Primary School, London

Tesla

T eslas are electric, driving with speed.

E lectric car, driving so clean.

S igned by the scientist Nikola Tesla.

L ikeable for someone who wants to go fast.

A ctually fast. Who wants to buy?

Elijah Nuamah (9)

Rosetta Primary School, London

Summer

S ummer is fun
U can go and smell the flowers
M e and my friends are going to the spring fair
M e and my friends love summer
E veryone enjoys the weather .
R oses are red.

Elissa Hassan (9)
Rosetta Primary School, London

The Razor Retires (Finally)

R un, before your brother shaves you bald.
A wful, you will look.
Z oom through the house.
O nly today, the razor retired.
R etired, yes, finally retired.

Mohammed Zayaan Hussain (9)
Rosetta Primary School, London

Donnie

D onnie is very smart
O nly good at football
N ice boy with amazing hair
N ice massive boy
I love football
E veryone support West Ham.

Donnie Marsh (9)
Rosetta Primary School, London

Nature

N ature is fun.

A nimals enjoy it.

T he plants grow easily.

U nder the sun you can see the beautiful world.

R ain falls down.

E ndless.

Rhema Odede (9)
Rosetta Primary School, London

Taco

T aco from out of the sky,
A ll I think about are tacos,
C ame from the sky, taco,
O ver my head, so yummy, yum yum taco.

Clinton Osakwe (9)
Rosetta Primary School, London

Leo

L eo is the best at throwing stuff in PE,

E very day he is playing football,

O n the job to help people around him.

Leo Munroe (9)

Rosetta Primary School, London

Silent Soarers Of The River Tale

Through the mountains high,
Splash through the river that reflects,
Curious and soaring above.

Keyaan Aryan Earla (8)
Rosetta Primary School, London

Space

Completely quiet, like space,
Never-ending like space,
Softly shining, great for stars moving.

Billy Ferrier (8)
Rosetta Primary School, London

Happy

H elpful
A wesome
P olite
P layful
Y oung.

Lyza Reddin (9) & Tre Guy (8)
Rosetta Primary School, London

Untitled

H elpful
A wesome
P layful
P olite
Y oung.

Jayzon Philpot Pierre (9)
Rosetta Primary School, London

Happy

H appy
A wesome
P olite
P layful
Y oung.

Maddison Candler (9) & Bernice
Rosetta Primary School, London

My Dog

My dog is small,
My dog is nice.
He plays all day,
And sleeps at night.

Deniz Nazim Gursul (9)
Rosetta Primary School, London

Wonders Of Nature

Beneath the sky, so vast and blue,
Lies a world of wonder, fresh and true.
Mountains stand tall, proud and wise,
Guarding secrets under skies.

The rivers dance with a joyful song,
Weaving through valleys, rushing along.
Their crystal waters, cool and pure,
Offer life, a timeless cure.

The forests hum with a gentle tune,
Leaves shimmering in the light of the moon.
Whispering winds through branches play
As creatures stir at the break of day.

Fields of flowers, a vibrant spread,
Blanket the Earth where angels tread.
Their fragrance sweet, their colours bright,
A masterpiece kissed by morning light.

Hikmah Lawal (9)
Sandbrook Community Primary School, Rochdale

All About Cheetahs

Cheetah, cheetah
Cat with spots
Such a skinny cat
With lots of dots.
If I challenged
A big fast cat
It would be impossible
To beat.

Bursts of speed, quite
A blast, cheetahs are
Always extremely
Fast.

The cheetah is a great
Big cat, but very quick
For all of that, she's
Cunning but she's gentle
Too, and if you're good
She's good to you.

Cheetah wins without
Trying, and it still
Is the fastest animal in
The world.

Mohamed Barry (9)
Sandbrook Community Primary School, Rochdale

The Weight Of Words

Sometimes at school,
It's not so bright.
When mean words hurt,
With all their might.
Bullying comes,
A shallow grey.
Making kids feel sad,
Every day.

But we can stand up,
Hand in hand,
To stop the bullies,
In this land.
Tell a teacher,
Speak up loud.
Let kindness be,
Our banner proud.

We'll spread some smiles,
And lend a friend,
So bullying's reign,
Will surely end.
With courage strong,
We'll make it right,

And fill the world,
With some happy light.

Amelia Khan Speak (9)
Sandbrook Community Primary School, Rochdale

The Couple And The True Hero

A hero is not the loudest,
Not always the strongest,
Not the one with the medal, or the flashing light.
A hero is the one who keeps going,
Step by step, the one who says,
"I'll help."

They don't run from fear,
They walk through it,
One breath,
One heartheat,
One brave choice.

A hero can be anyone,
A sister,
A friend,
A kid in the playground who says,
"Stop, that's not right."

Alyaannah Shaikh (9)
Sandbrook Community Primary School, Rochdale

Planet Jupiter

In the sky so big and bright,
A majestic sight.
With swirling clouds of orange and brown,
The largest planet wearing a crown.

With its great red spot, a storm so wide,
Roars with winds that swirl and glide,
Sixty moons dance around its gleam,
A gas giant, big as a dream.

With rings so faint, a gentle show,
It's *Jupiter*, the king of the cosmos,
We all know!

Raza (9)
Sandbrook Community Primary School, Rochdale

The Lines Of Nature

Birds are flying,
Rivers are flowing,
The flowers are shining,
Ducks are swimming,
Bunnies are hopping,
The sun is shining,
The waves are crashing.

Cheetahs are running,
Leaves are falling,
Ants are marching,
The sharks are hunting,
The grass is glowing,
Trees are growing,
Lions are roaring,
Wolves are howling.

And anything I can imagine.

Hanan Mudassar (9)
Sandbrook Community Primary School, Rochdale

The N And M World

In the galaxy, N and M play,
We hop aboard a spaceship,
We're going to Teddy Planet.
Buckle your seatbelt and put on your helmet,
Here comes the countdown,
Ten, nine, eight, seven, six, five, four, three, two, one,
blast-off!
We're very excited to go to Teddy Planet,
Because we love it so so much,
And we love it there.

Nevaeh-Rose McCulloch (9)
Sandbrook Community Primary School, Rochdale

All About Space

You look up at the sky
And the sun shines bright like you
You go up to space
And everyone loves you
Everyone sees the high trees
And you are a high tree
An alien is green
An alien is white
An alien is red
Saturn has a ring just like you
In your head, that controls your brain.

Holly Holmes Smithes (9)
Sandbrook Community Primary School, Rochdale

A Summer's Day

S plashing in the perfect paddling pool. Yay!

U mbrellas for shade to eat ice cream under. Scrumptious!

M emories and music whilst dancing in the sun. Woo!

M ango smoothies with friends. Yummy!

E nding the evening with goodbyes and hugs. "See you later!"

R elaxing after a hot day. Ahh.

S cranning popsicles and burgers from the barbecue. Tasty!

D andelions dancing in the light wind. Beautiful!

A pples all ripe on the fruit tree. Healthy!

Y ou can love summer, no matter who you are. Bye! Summer is lovely. Fun times!

Ella Yates (10)
Shevington Vale Primary School, Appley Bridge

Animals

A dventures of amazing animals share the pufferfish ball.

N aturally nice zookeepers water the perfect plants for the amazing animals.

I ndependent intelligent dolphins dive into the water and amaze people with the pufferfish ball.

M agnificent lions are demolishing and destroying the enclosure together, quicker than ever!

A pretty penguin rolling around. The winter snow falls. All are playing with the pufferfish ball.

L ady lions are calming the males, as the sun shines, before returning to dark.

S pecial surprises and wonder from our incredible wildlife.

Rosa Blinkhorn (9)
Shevington Vale Primary School, Appley Bridge

Waddles And Daisy

All through spring and summer, Waddles and Daisy went on an adventure. They saw a penguin holding a staff. His name was Callam. They waved hello, then waved bye.

They wandered by a meadow and they found a place to sleep for the night. They fell asleep in their cosy den and dreamed of unicorns and rainbows.

When Waddles woke up, Daisy was nowhere to be seen. She started to cry and sob until she saw a penguin. The penguin was holding Daisy.

She wiped away her tears and ran to the penguin. It was Callam. He said he saw her flying by, so he caught her.

So they waddled back to their den.

Sophia Koskinas (9)
Shevington Vale Primary School, Appley Bridge

Growing Up

G rowing up instils fear in me,

R ough red spots bursting through my skin.

O ily skin and greasy hair that everyone can see,

W hile pretty, popular girls don't let me in!

I nside the hurt used to bring me down,

N ow people are sorry for being so mean.

G rowing up is an important part of life, so don't frown!

U nhappy people don't get far, so be a happy teen.

P art of life is growing up, so I'm going to do it with a smile!

Niamh Latham (10)

Shevington Vale Primary School, Appley Bridge

Space

The moon glistens in the night sky,
Sometimes the stars die,
Look around, you'll see your family,
Look up, you'll see your galaxy.

The constellations might align,
Look closer, you'll see them shine,
Jupiter is made of gas,
The sun holds a lot of mass.

Look inside a telescope,
Mars has water... we hope,
The stats shine like a dime,
Sun rays hit Earth from through a maze.

Ollie Anderson (10)
Shevington Vale Primary School, Appley Bridge

Winter

W arm weather has gone, but here comes the snow.

I nside is cosy and warm, wrapped up in a blanket, sitting by the fire.

N ice, nice children get excited because Santa's nearly here.

T insel, trees and stars on top, Christmas is near.

E veryone is exchanging gifts, and the children are making snow angels.

R inging ringing bells, the carollers shall come.

Lucy Lavery (10)

Shevington Vale Primary School, Appley Bridge

Animals

A nimals are cute and fluffy

N ever ugly and no fear

I nside is nice and warm

M eerkats roam around the desert happily

A penguin rolling around happily in the snow in winter

L ovely lions under the savanna trees

S ome animals live in the forest and some don't. Animals are wild, and some are not.

Madison Ascroft (9)

Shevington Vale Primary School, Appley Bridge

The Shark

Down in the depths
Of the sea,
Lurks a monster,
Scarier than a monkey.

It hides behind big rocks,
Waiting to find its prey,
And then it jumps out.
Guess that won't survive another day.

It... is called the shark.
It has gills,
It is also dark grey,
It also has a lot of kills.
The shark.

Blake Bristow (10)
Shevington Vale Primary School, Appley Bridge

Friendship Grows With Nature

F riends by my side, always there
R ays of sunshine, laughter in the air
I n the arms of nature, we find solace
E very moment shared, a precious embrace
N ature's beauty, a backdrop to our bend
D elighting in each other, we respond
S avouring the memories we create
H appiness and love, never too late
I n every adventure, as life carries on
P recious and timeless, it's friendship we earn

G rowing up together, hand in hand.
R eaching for the stars, a united band
O vercoming challenges, we stand tall
W oven together, we'll never fall
S miling faces, forever free.

And life's a puzzle for you and me.

Labeebah Odumosu (9)
Wath Victoria Primary School, Wath Upon Dearne

YoungWriters®
Est. 1991

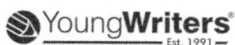

YOUNG WRITERS INFORMATION

We hope you have enjoyed reading this book – and that you will continue to in the coming years.

If you're the parent or family member of an enthusiastic poet or story writer, do visit our website **www.youngwriters.co.uk/subscribe** and sign up to receive news, competitions, writing challenges and tips, activities and much, much more! There's lots to keep budding writers motivated!

If you would like to order further copies of this book, or any of our other titles, then please give us a call or order via your online account.

Young Writers
Remus House
Coltsfoot Drive
Peterborough
PE2 9BF
(01733) 890066
info@youngwriters.co.uk

Join in the conversation!
Tips, news, giveaways and much more!

f YoungWritersUK **X** YoungWritersCW
⊙ youngwriterscw **♪** youngwriterscw

**Scan to watch
the video!**